MORE LIFE'S LITTLE DESTRUCTION BOOK

A Parody

Charles Sherwood Dane

WARNER BOOKS

A *Warner* Book

First published in the United States in 1993
by St. Martin's Press

First published in Great Britain in 1994
by Warner Books

A CIP catalogue record for this book is available from the British Library.

ISBN 0 7515 1089 0

Photoset in North Wales by Derek Doyle & Associates, Mold, Clwyd.
Printed and bound in Great Britain by
Clays Ltd St Ives plc

Warner Books
A Division of
Little, Brown and Company (UK) Limited
Brettenham House
Lancaster Place
London WC2E 7EN

INTRODUCTION

All right, all right. We heard you! All the clamour for this new collection of mean and rotten ways to make everyone miserable. It just goes to prove what we've been saying all along: you can't have too much of a bad thing.

Maybe we've softened but we've added two additional bonuses for you:

1) Little White Lies you can tell to cover your you know what, and

2) A bunch of ways to make yourself totally miserable. We call these Self Destructions.

Now go out there and make us proud!

We reluctantly must thank again all who contributed to this little lampoon. They are, in no particular order, Ned Bienemann, Sheree Bykofsky, David Dinin, Christopher Fargis, Paul Fargis, Victoria Gallucci, Caroline McKeldin, Adam O'Conner, Lea Bayers Rapp, Tricia Reinus, Celine Texier Rose, Wendy Silbert, and Jennifer Weis.

513 ◆ Carry a grudge.

514 ◆ Wait until you're in the voting booth to decide.

515 ◆ Cross your leg over and keep shaking your foot.

516 ◆ Emulate Bart Simpson.

517 ◆ Whatever it is, be against it.

518 ◆ Power Trip.

519 ◆ Be first on the bus, then grope around for change.

520 ◆ Bring an uninvited guest to the wedding.

521 ◆ Make sure the car behind you catches the red light.

522 ◆ Pretend you didn't hear the question.

523 ◆ Before you give that hearty handshake, sneeze into your hand.

524 ◆ Tell kids, 'Sleep tight; don't let the bed bugs bite.'

525 ◆ When you do something bad, use someone else's name.

526 ◆ When you're in a foreign country, refuse to speak the language.

527 ◆ When the collection plate is passed to you, help yourself.

528 ◆ At a convention, stare at people's badges when you talk to them.

529 ◆ Assign blame.

530 ◆ Raise your voice so that people who don't speak English will understand.

531 ◆ Develop a truly blank look.

532 ◆ Drool.

533 ◆ Get drunk before PTA meetings.

534 ◆ Staple cheque to paying-in slip before posting.

535 ◆ Walk on freshly seeded grass.

536 ◆ Eavesdrop.

537 ◆ Blow your horn as soon as the light turns green.

538 ◆ Blow your stack.

539 ◆ Paint your fingernails on the aeroplane.

540 ◆ Seduce a superior, and then claim sexual harassment.

541 ◆ House an illegal alien.

542 ◆ Turn up the volume on late movies.

543 ◆ Rub everyone up the wrong way.

544 ◆ Actually chill out.

545 ◆ Begin a job interview by asking about the holidays.

546 ◆ Poke kids playfully in their belly-buttons.

547 ◆ Tell your hostess her dishes are dirty.

548 ◆ Brush your hair in the kitchen.

549 ◆ Dampen spirits and edit out joy.

550 ◆ Serve runny eggs.

551 ◆ Use a loudhailer to call the ref obscene names.

552 ◆ Strive to be politically perfect, not just politically correct.

553 ◆ Go to the concert with a hacking cough.

554 ◆ When the pianist pauses, applaud.

555 ◆ Scratch your crotch in public.

556 ◆ Breastfeed your twins at the stadium.

557 ◆ Be one of the guys who just doesn't get it.

558 ◆ Show people where they went wrong.

559 ◆ Stare at the chests of big-breasted
women.

560 ◆ Insist you were there first.

561 ◆ Remember, all's fair in love and war.

562 ◆ Convert to humanism in church.

563 ◆ Send gifts C.O.D.

564 ◆ Be redundant, time and time again.

565 ◆ Talk in rhyme all the time.

566 ◆ Never, never change your routine.

567 ◆ Look busy.

568 ◆ Leave lipstick on his collar.

569 ◆ Outline his bald spot with your finger.

570 ◆ If you sprinkle when you tinkle, just leave it.

571 ◆ Pull the rug out from under someone.

572 ◆ Collect Sweet 'n Low from restaurants.

573 ◆ Tell your friend about her surprise party.

574 ◆ Have all the answers.

575 ◆ Suggest to mourners that they cheer up and look on the bright side.

576 ◆ Shuffle someone else's alphabetical file.

577 ◆ Tickle people.

578 ◆ Say you're sorry in a cheerful, lilting voice.

579 ◆ Slap people on the back.

580 ◆ Bite into the piece of fruit before offering it to someone else.

581 ◆ Show up late.

582 ◆ Leave early.

583 ◆ Ride your bike on crowded pavements.

584 ◆ Make notes on linen napkins in restaurants.

585 ◆ Recommend that she shave her legs more often.

586 ◆ Crash your way into a parking space.

587 ◆ Be in contempt of court.

588 ◆ Bear false witness.

589 ◆ 'Shoot' the messenger.

590 ◆ Leave your name in wet cement.

591 ◆ Break hearts, wind, and rules.

592 ◆ Bring pizza and beer to the Intensive Care Unit.

593 ◆ Tell your children that babies come from storks.

594 ◆ When you get close to celebrities, rip off a piece of their clothing.

595 ◆ Contradict your spouse loudly in public.

596 ◆ The phonier the better.

597 ◆ Ask very personal questions.

598 ◆ Take advantage of everyone.

599 ◆ Play mind games.

600 ◆ Don't replace the toilet paper roll.

601 ◆ Preach gloom and doom.

602 ◆ Throw your money around.

603 ◆ Leave other people's business cards in telephone boxes.

604 ◆ Give your friends' names to mailing lists and telephone sales people.

605 ◆ Insist that people search for things that aren't lost.

606 ◆ Get one of those 'Theme from The Godfather' car horns.

607 ◆ Practise misanthropy and misogyny.

608 ◆ Go ahead even when you know you are making a mistake.

609 ◆ Go to bed angry.

610 ◆ If you can't bedazzle them with your brilliance, baffle them with your bullshit.

611 ◆ Try getting away with murder.

612 ◆ If that doesn't work, try mayhem.

613 ◆ Suggest nose jobs to your friends.

614 ◆ Don't know and don't care.

615 ◆ Lash out at people who are only trying to help.

616 ◆ An ounce of cure is worth a pound of prevention.

617 ◆ Mail the postcards after you get back from vacation.

618 ◆ Delve into things that are none of your business.

619 ◆ Fill out deposit slips at the cashier's window.

620 ◆ See how tall and yellow your lawn can get.

621 ◆ Touch the tip of your shoes against the heels of the person in the queue in front of you.

622 ◆ Create warring factions in your family.

623 ◆ Ask them to name all 54 flavours, then order vanilla.

624 ◆ Believe you are above the law.

625 ◆ Lean back and look at your visitor through a thin, cold smile.

626 ◆ No need to say please or thank you.

627 ◆ Love is never having to say you're sorry.

628 ◆ Moan and groan.

629 ◆ Doubletalk.

630 ◆ Count your chickens before they are conceived.

631 ◆ Play monkey in the middle with your little niece.

632 ◆ Split the bill only when your meal costs more.

633 ◆ When you scratch his back, avoid the spot that itches.

634 ◆ Reserve the sunlounger and then go swimming all day.

635 ◆ Finish people's sentences for them.

636 ◆ Toss and turn when you're sleeping over.

637 ◆ Serve children blue cheese dressing.

638 ◆ You're right. The world does revolve around you.

639 ◆ Put a video camera in the employee washroom.

640 ◆ Make a visitor stand.

641 ◆ Elbow your way through a crowd.

642 ◆ Concentrate on trivia.

643 ◆ Don't hesitate: show the contempt you feel.

644 ◆ Humiliate someone when you need to establish control.

645 ◆ Stop and stare at accidents.

646 ◆ Tell everyone to prove it.

647 ◆ Prop your feet up on the boss's desk.

648 ◆ Borrow receipts to take to the IRS audit.

649 ◆ Slip a foul word by the personal number plate censors.

650 ◆ Weave in and out of traffic just for fun.

651 ◆ Never let it be good enough.

652 ◆ Always play devil's advocate.

653 ◆ Wear a string bikini at the gym.

654 ◆ Rapidly recite your address to someone who is writing it down.

655 ◆ Stop as soon as you get off the escalator.

656 ◆ Tell your colleague you overheard a plan to fire him.

657 ◆ Leave a note from the tooth fairy, 'Out of cash'.

658 ◆ Tell him that you bought a false Rolex just like his.

659 ◆ Point out that her necklace emphasises her double chin.

660 ◆ Allow every man his say, then contradict it.

661 ◆ Invite them for dinner and don't be home.

662 ◆ When you're really needed, leave town.

663 ◆ Eat garlic bread before your dental appointment.

664 ◆ Leave the soap on the shower floor.

665 ◆ Pollute.

666 ◆ Lie in confession.

667 ◆ Tell tall tales.

668 ◆ Comment on the contents of your host's bathroom cabinet.

669 ◆ Leave your messes for someone else to clean up.

670 ◆ Recommend an inept financial advisor.

671 ◆ Entertain flight passengers with crash stories.

672 ◆ Toss paper towels in the public toilet.

673 ◆ Adjust the reception while he's watching the big game.

674 ◆ Blow your nose at the dinner table.

675 ◆ Pull lint from his belly-button.

676 ◆ Wipe off your eye make-up on the guest towels.

677 ◆ Tell a sick person about people you know who died.

678 ◆ Squeak chalk across the blackboard.

679 ◆ Tap their glassware to see if it rings.

680 ◆ When you meet people, make it clear you're sizing them up.

681 ◆ Don't come when you're called.

682 ◆ Keep on talking and talking and talking.

683 ◆ Have a cow.

684 ◆ Cheat at snooker.

685 ◆ Always aim low.

686 ◆ Pick your nose and eat it.

687 ◆ When the doctor says, 'Cough', spit.

688 ◆ Kiss and tell.

689 ◆ Act like a whore in front of your in-laws.

690 ◆ Ignore your call waiting.

691 ◆ 'Borrow' other people's pens and pencils.

692 ◆ Mispronounce a colleague's name – for eleven years.

693 ◆ Leave a few stones unturned.

694 ◆ When your colleague asks if you like his new haircut, cough.

695 ◆ Speed up after you pass the radar.

696 ◆ Pop a child's balloon.

697 ◆ Tell filthy jokes.

698 ◆ Hover aggressively over hors d'oeuvres.

699 ◆ Throw recyclables into the regular trash.

700 ◆ Go ahead: ask what your country can do for you.

701 ◆ Always say never.

702 ◆ Eat ice cream in front of the children and don't share.

703 ◆ Plead poverty.

704 ◆ Leave a long message on your answering machine.

705 ◆ Fall asleep on jury duty.

706 ◆ Ask people how they got their limp.

707 ◆ Fire well before you see the whites of their eyes.

708 ◆ Groan when you sit down.

709 ◆ Groan when you stand up.

710 ◆ Do don't's and don't do do's.

711 ◆ Say 'uh-oh' a lot.

712 ◆ Don't give an inch.

713 ◆ Try on underwear in stores.

714 ◆ Name your new baby Rothschild.

715 ◆ Return from the office loo exclaiming:
'Boy, that Feen-a-Mint really works.'

716 ◆ Examine your Kleenex carefully after use.

717 ◆ Confuse first and second wives.

718 ◆ Leave roller skates on the stairs.

719 ◆ After the first person gives you directions, turn and ask someone else.

720 ◆ If an excuse is good enough to use once, it's good enough to use again.

721 ◆ Ask people to tell you again how their pet died.

722 ◆ In the changing room, stare at people as they undress.

723 ◆ Knock on limousine windows and peer inside.

724 ◆ Tell new neighbours that the neighbourhood's gone downhill.

725 ◆ Dial a wrong number in the middle of the night – twice.

726 ◆ Squeeze your boyfriends' pimples.

727 ◆ A little white lie never hurt anyone.

LIFE'S LITTLE WHITE LIES AND EXCUSES

Knowing how to tell a little lie is integral to getting by in life....

728 ◆ Read my lips.

729 ◆ I'll ask my manager, but I doubt it.

730 ◆ Gee, I guess the invitation was just lost in the mail.

731 ◆ I thought you said you would take care of it.

732 ◆ I'm serious, you look great in that hat.

733 ◆ Have you lost weight?

734 ◆ No problem.

735 ◆ I'll call you.

736 ◆ Take my word for it.

737 ◆ Relax, nothing will go wrong.

738 ◆ Money back guarantee.

739 ◆ I never got the fax.

740 ◆ I'm not angry; I'm not mad.

741 ◆ I'm about to go into a meeting.

742 ◆ The traffic was really bad.

743 ◆ You'll have to pay because I forgot my wallet.

744 ◆ I rarely drink this much.

745 ◆ David's parents said that he could.

746 ◆ I had to go to a funeral.

747 ◆ I'll keep your c.v. on file.

748 ◆ This wrinkle cream actually reverses ageing.

749 ◆ You're too good for me.

750 ◆ This is my last piece of cake.

751 ◆ I'd do it for you.

752 ◆ I'm washing my hair that week.

753 ◆ One adult and four children, please.

754 ◆ Next time it's on me.

755 ◆ I promise not to tell anyone – ever.

756 ◆ My answering machine is broken, and I never got the message.

757 ◆ I was just going to call you.

758 ◆ You can trust me.

759 ◆ This hurts me more than it hurts you.

760 ◆ No offence.

761 ◆ Let me make this perfectly clear.

762 ◆ I am not a crook.

763 ◆ May the best person win.

764 ◆ I'm a size 10.

765 ◆ 'All the taste of butter without the calories.'

766 ◆ This is for your own good.

767 ◆ You'll see, this medicine tastes just like cherry syrup.

768 ◆ I never saw him before in my life.

769 ◆ It was the wrong kind of snow.

770 ◆ Honey, I have to work late.

771 ◆ He hit me first.

772 ◆ It was good for me, too.

773 ◆ It's not the money; I love working in the legal profession.

774 ◆ I hear my mother calling me.

775 ◆ Actually, I like the taste of tofu.

776 ◆ It feels so good to be single again.

777 ◆ It's one-of-a-kind.

778 ◆ It's nothing personal, I'm just not interested in dating right now.

779 ◆ It's so simple a child can do it.

780 ◆ I'm really glad you got that off your chest.

781 ◆ I'm just on my way out the door.

782 ◆ My grandmother died. (Again.)

783 ◆ I must be losing my memory.

784 ◆ It's in mint condition.

785 ◆ I knew that.

786 ◆ I never eat. Why am I so fat?

787 ◆ Oh, I thought it was tomorrow night.

788 ◆ This time, I mean it.

789 ◆ You're my favourite mother-in-law.

790 ◆ I never said that.

791 ◆ I won't make the same mistake again.

792 ◆ I was never told.

793 ◆ You're my best friend in the whole wide world.

794 ◆ I love you.

795 ◆ I love you, too.

796 ◆ If I had to lose, I'm glad you won.

797 ◆ The dog ate my homework.

798 ◆ Please don't take this the wrong way, but....

799 ◆ Sorry, my car broke down.

800 ◆ I didn't feel a thing.

801 ◆ Studies show....

802 ◆ Easy to assemble.

803 ◆ I was only teasing.

804 ◆ I'll be right with you.

805 ◆ We're just good friends.

806 ◆ I followed directions.

807 ◆ I'm not lying. Honest.

808 ◆ That's the cutest baby I've ever seen.

809 ◆ I can't believe that's a toupee – it looks so natural.

810 ◆ I have no idea how this got broken.

811 ◆ I'd love to see more baby pictures.

812 ◆ I'll just go back to sleep for five more minutes.

813 ◆ I'm just smoking to keep my weight down.

814 ◆ I love to have the grandchildren visit.

815 ◆ Honey, that was the best meatloaf I've ever had.

816 ◆ I really only listen to Radio 3.

817 ◆ Back in the old days, I was a handsome devil.

818 ◆ I don't mind sleeping on the floor.

819 ◆ No, I don't mind staying until 9 P.M.

820 ◆ Diet shakes are so satisfying.

821 ◆ I didn't want it, anyway.

822 ◆ I'd love to stay and help, but I have to be somewhere.

823 ◆ Keep driving; I think I know where we are now.

824 ◆ I'd like to still be friends.

825 ◆ It's an honour to meet you, Prime Minister.

826 ◆ What grey hair?

827 ◆ There's a swimsuit to flatter every figure.

828 ◆ My home is your home – stay as long as you like.

829 ◆ I've chosen a bridesmaid dress that you can wear again.

830 ◆ 'Handsome, athletic, intelligent, sensitive, SWM seeks....'

831 ◆ Tastes just like homemade.

832 ◆ ☺ Have a nice day.

LIFE'S LITTLE SELF DESTRUCTIONS

When you're through ragging on everyone else,
there's only one person left to torture....

833 ◆ Apologize even if you didn't do anything.

834 ◆ Apologize for living.

835 ◆ Apologize for apologizing.

836 ◆ Live in a constant state of denial.

837 ◆ Don't fasten your seat belt – you're only going for a quick drive.

838 ◆ Forget to sign your Christmas cards.

839 ◆ Lock your keys in the car.

840 ◆ Monopolize the most boring person at a dinner party.

841 ◆ Step off the kerb without checking for puddles.

842 ◆ Buy a budgerigar for your cat.

843 ◆ As you introduce your husband, forget his name.

844 ◆ Shoot a whole roll without any film.

845 ◆ Break a mirror.

846 ◆ Stand on rickety old chairs.

847 ◆ Need to be in two places at once.

848 ◆ Tell your friends to drop by your summer home any weekend.

849 ◆ Leap before you look.

850 ◆ Change your mind.

851 ◆ Change it back.

852 ◆ Delay until it's too late.

853 ◆ Write a nasty letter to the Inland Revenue.

854 ◆ Bawl out a policeman while he's writing you a ticket.

855 ◆ Suggest meeting your blind date at a topless bar.

856 ◆ Describe your sex life to your in-laws.

857 ◆ If something goes wrong, eat a whole bag of potato chips.

858 ◆ If you go up to the limit on your credit card, get another one.

859 ◆ Bite your nails while you are waiting.

860 ◆ If at first you don't succeed, cry.

861 ◆ If you don't come from a dysfunctional family, make one up.

862 ◆ Unload your problems on your kids.

863 ◆ Compare yourself to others for that greater than/less than feeling.

864 ◆ List your membership in AA on your c.v.

865 ◆ Start that long drive home when you're drowsy.

866 ◆ When the relationship is definitely over, try to make it work again.

867 ◆ When he cheats on you, make it up to him.

868 ◆ See an ineffectual psychiatrist for years.

869 ◆ Support your friend's coke habit.

870 ◆ Hide the bottle in plain sight.

871 ◆ Let every stranger control your life.

872 ♦ Say yes when you mean no.

873 ♦ Buy yet another diet book.

874 ♦ If you're not the oppressor, be the victim.

875 ♦ Work for your ex.

876 ◆ Spend all your holidays with your parents.

877 ◆ Be a wallflower.

878 ◆ Walk with your eyes down.

879 ◆ Nap during your therapy session.

880 ◆ Always let people go ahead of you in the queue.

881 ◆ Wake up and smell the manure.

882 ◆ Rationalize away your problems.

883 ◆ Make up your mind and don't change.

884 ◆ Never look people in the eye.

885 ◆ Wear white when you have your period.

886 ◆ At the Bingo hall buy a vowel that's been called already.

887 ♦ Spend more than you earn.

888 ◆ Agree with everyone else all the time.

889 ◆ Make important decisions by flipping a coin.

890 ◆ Tell different lies to different people until you forget what the truth is.

891 ◆ Tell people you're recovering.

892 ◆ Only see one solution.

893 ◆ Ask people who don't like you for help.

894 ◆ Don't feel your feelings.

895 ◆ Heave a sigh and do what they want anyway.

896 ◆ Be assertive ... NOT!

897 ◆ Always mount a horse on its right side.

898 ◆ Pull on an itchy label and rip the collar.

899 ◆ The night before your big job interview, set your alarm clock for 6:00 P.M.

900 ◆ Buy expensive things on impulse.

901 ◆ Sit directly down on the public toilet seat without looking first.

902 ◆ If you're ever lucky enough to meet the Queen, give her a big hug.

903 ◆ Order pesto fettucini with lobster at a job interview lunch.

904 ◆ Forget your passport.

905 ◆ After the second date, move in together.

906 ◆ Wear pastel blue leisure suits and white loafers.

907 ◆ Pack heavy groceries into flimsy bags.

908 ◆ Enter a beauty pageant.

909 ◆ Let life pass you by.

910 ◆ Ignore expiry dates on prescription bottles.

911 ◆ Blame yourself for everyone else's problems.

912 ◆ Turn off your computer before saving your work.

913 ◆ Load up on goodies for 'unexpected company'.

914 ◆ Tape a stupid TV show over your all-time favourite movie.

915 ◆ Machine wash your silk dress.

916 ◆ Invite your mother-in-law for a visit when your mother is already ensconced in the guest room.

917 ◆ Sit next to the fattest person on a long distance coach journey.

918 ◆ Believe him when he says his wife doesn't understand him.

919 ◆ Flush your diamond engagement ring down the toilet to prove you're angry with him.

920 ◆ Save that snapshot that makes you look like a cow.

921 ◆ Call him every ten minutes.

922 ◆ Send an expensive wedding gift but forget to include your name.

923 ◆ Leave your sex toys around when the cleaning lady comes.

924 ◆ Bring your talkative friend along to a silent retreat.

925 ◆ Try a complicated new recipe for your last minute dinner party.

926 ◆ Call in sick and then go lunch-time shopping right near your office.

927 ◆ Just for a change, walk home down the dark, narrow alley.

928 ◆ Jump in the shower with no towel in sight.

929 ◆ Order a diet cola with a huge scoop of ice cream.

930 ◆ So you're allergic, eat it anyway.

931 ◆ Lend your friend money just one more time.

932 ◆ Arrive at the airport five minutes before your international flight.

933 ◆ Ask a chronic complainer, 'How are you?'

934 ◆ Rent the flat over a night club.

935 ◆ Decide to attend a college you've never visited.

936 ◆ Flaunt your infidelity.

937 ◆ Forget to check the petrol gauge.

938 ◆ Forget to lock the toilet door.

939 ◆ Add chlorine bleach to the coloured wash.

940 ◆ Attempt to break up a fight on the underground.

941 ◆ Buy running shoes without trying them on.

942 ◆ Sit home on a Saturday night and wait for his call.

943 ◆ Clean your loaded handgun.

944 ◆ In front of the children.

945 ◆ Assume the bank NEVER makes a mistake.

946 ◆ Keep your money under your mattress.

947 ◆ Be the designated driver when drinks are on the house.

948 ◆ Enjoy a huge meal before you ride the roller coaster.

949 ◆ Call 0898 numbers and talk for hours.

950 ◆ Threaten your kids with, 'Wait until Daddy gets home'.

951 ◆ Let your make-up dry out – especially blue eyeshadow.

952 ◆ Belabour a point.

953 ◆ Belabour a point.

954 ◆ Talk toofast.

955 ◆ Don't pay your bookie.

956 ◆ Kiss a frog and hope it becomes a prince.

957 ◆ Talk only about yourself on a first date.

958 ◆ Drink the water in Mexico.

959 ◆ Drink the contents of your finger bowl at a formal state dinner.

960 ◆ Get dressed in the dark.

961 ◆ Just say 'Yes.'

962 ◆ Ask to see more wedding pictures.

963 ◆ Eat more fried foods.

964 ◆ Pick your teeth with the
business card a client has
just handed you.

965 ◆ Pay extra for the one-hour dry-cleaning service and come back three weeks later to pick it up.

966 ◆ Ask your lawyer to contact the jurors to improve the odds of winning your case.

967 ◆ Volunteer to be the 'before' model in diet ads.

968 ◆ Don't name your computer files.

969 ◆ Choose your career on the advice of a psychic.

970 ◆ Correct your boss in front of his peers.

971 ◆ Let the toddlers have as much chocolate as they want.

972 ◆ Post important letters without a stamp.

973 ◆ Volunteer your house for the wedding reception.

974 ◆ Obsess over a celebrity.

975 ◆ Drink coffee close to bedtime.

976 ◆ Tear up a photo of the Pope on national television.

977 ◆ Binge and purge.

978 ◆ Look for true love in the personal ads.

979 ◆ Tuck your skirt into your tights after going to the loo.

980 ◆ Make a pass at your sister's husband.

981 ◆ Joke about shooting the Queen while queuing for the Buck House tour.

982 ◆ Rely on your memory.

983 ◆ Load up on prunes before a hot date.

984 ◆ Stick the bubbling hot pizza right in your mouth.

985 ◆ Plead ignorance.

986 ◆ Walk under a ladder.

987 ◆ Stop using four letter words and try labels like cretin, doofus, and schmuck.

988 ◆ Get a job making cold calls at meal times.

989 ◆ Over-react.

990 ◆ Wear tights that sag.

991 ◆ Be co-dependent.

992 ◆ Make promises you can't possibly keep.

993 ◆ Miss two hire purchase payments.

994 ◆ Toilet train her before she's ready.

995 ◆ Pick up the bill all the time.

996 ◆ Play with fire.

997 ◆ When he asks for all the details, tell him.

998 ◆ Ask for trouble.

999 ◆ Play hard to get when you want to get got.

1000 ◆ Bake like a flounder in the hot summer sun.

1001 ◆ Hang your handbag over the back of your chair in crowded restaurants.

1002 ◆ Put the wrong letters in the wrong envelopes.

1003 ◆ Play with your vegetables.

1004 ◆ Cut in front of London taxis.

1005 ◆ Whenever your child whines for a new toy, buy it.

1006 ◆ Leave the tube of black shoe polish near the toothpaste.

1007 ◆ Look on the dark side.

1008 ◆ Cross your fingers when you tell a lie.

1009 ◆ Ward off evil spirits with garlic.

1010 ◆ Let people wipe their feet on you.

1011 ◆ Have the foggiest idea.

1012 ◆ Step out on the ledge to wash the high-rise windows.

1013 ◆ Don't do today what you can put off until tomorrow.

1014 ◆ Press your luck.

1015 ◆ Skate on thin ice.

1016 ◆ Judge a book by its cover.

1017 ◆ Don't replace the spare.

1018 ◆ Open mouth. Insert foot.

1019 ◆ Wear diamonds, gold necklaces, and furs on the underground.

1020 ◆ Try to please all of the people all of the time.

1021 ◆ Seek out negative influences.

1022 ◆ Believe everything you read.

1023 ◆ Mull it over in the middle of the night.

1024 ◆ Vote Conservative.

1025 ◆ Break up; go back; break up; go back.

1026 ◆ Go to work with a little cotton wool on your chin.

1027 ◆ Keep imagining everything else that can go wrong.

1028 ◆ Ask for a haircut when you want a trim.

1029 ◆ Insist on having the last word.